Letters in Silence

The Lost Letters of James King

Brought to Light by Omari Vale

CCP

CROWN CIPHER
PUBLISHING

For permissions, contact:
Crown Cipher Publishing
crowncipherpublishing.com

ISBN (Paperback): 979-8-9994700-8-9
ISBN (Ebook): 979-8-9994700-7-2

First Edition: 2025

Cover design by Crown Cipher Publishing
Interior design by Crown Cipher Publishing

A Crown Cipher Publishing Release
We protect this F**king House

Printed in the United States of America

Preface

What you hold in your hands is only a fragment.

There are hundreds of letters, poems, and notes—some captured digitally, many scribbled in notebooks and across scraps of paper. From that vast collection, only a small selection has been drawn here. They are not arranged in any particular order of time, but chosen to reveal the phases of love as they were lived: radiance, fracture, wound, echo.

Nothing has been rewritten or softened. Each piece stands as it was when first composed, many years ago—raw, jagged, and unfiltered. The only addition is the Dedication, a mark of reverence before the silence begins.

These letters are not polished poems, nor staged performances. They are confessions brought into the light, fragments of ruin that would not stay buried.

And while this book stands alone, it also offers something more. For those who have ever wondered about the complicated man known as James King—his brilliance, his torment, his impossible hunger—this is him at his most raw.

—Omari Vale

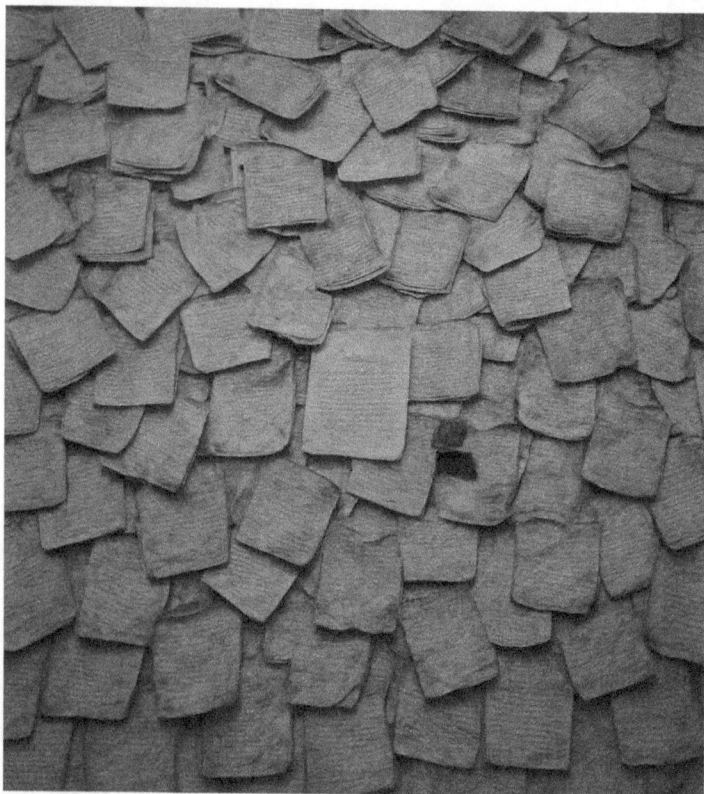

Table of Contents

Dedication

To Love—

You were the first to wound me.
Before betrayal wore a human face, before silence
belonged to a voice I knew,
it was you who carved me open. You dressed yourself in
radiance,
whispered promises that tasted like eternity,
and then taught me that eternity is a lie.

You split me without blade,
bled me without touch,
and left me worshiping ghosts.

You are the hush that answers when I beg.
You are the shadow pressed against my ribs when I
cannot breathe.
You are the echo that laughs when I whisper prayers into
nothing.

This book belongs to you.

Every page is your altar.

Every line is your scripture.

Every scar is your signature written in me.

You damned me.

You ruined me.

You hollowed me until all that remained was hunger for your absence.

And still, I kneel.

And still, I bleed.

And still, I call you holy.

Part I – The Radiance

Every bright thing bargains with a shadow.

Genesis of Love

My Love,

What is this wonder? This unexplainable surge that makes me lose myself in the gaze of your eyes—eyes that look back at me as if I am worth looking at. No one has ever looked at me this way. And now that you do, I am undone.

What is this feeling? Is it too much, too soon? My heart overflows, pretending is impossible. It feels like shallow water could drown me, and yet the depth of this love does not terrify—it baptizes me.

I cannot wait for the phone to ring, though I try to play it cool. The moment I hear your voice, I am unmade. How can something cost nothing, yet feel so priceless? How can it be free, and yet demand everything?

This is not a mother's love—it is another universe. I

would die for another taste. I thought only religion could feel this good, but you have made my soul kneel in worship. Is that why they say all beautiful things must have tragedy? Yet I feel no tragedy in you. Not now, not ever.

Is it too early to offer you my heart? Too early to burn down the world for you? I want to keep this pure, unsullied. I want to preserve the holiness of what I feel before silence stains it. You are too perfect to be real, and yet here you are.

Can I share this letter with you? Will it bring you joy to read it, as it brings me joy to write it? Am I allowed to confess that I am overwhelmed—that your name on my lips makes me hide tears I cannot explain? They tell me not to say love so soon, but my mind does not govern this. My heart is sovereign, and it already bows to you.

I have nothing to give you but myself. No wealth, no crown, no sanctuary—only a scarred heart in a trembling box. If I hand it to you, will you kiss it for every wound it has carried?

All I have seen before is betrayal, arguments, lies—wars disguised as love. Yet in you, I see the impossible. I want to be so good to you, if you only look twice. I beg you—see the love spilling over me.

They say everything has a price, even those three small words. But if I cannot say them now, then let me at least whisper this truth: I have never known optimism until you. Never believed in radiance until now.

This is my genesis.
This is love.

Always,
Me

What if you don't love me back?
My radiance turns to ruin.
I would drown in silence—
dying not from absence,
but from your indifference.

Joy in Your Hands

My Love,

To love, and to be loved back—what wonder is greater?

Each time you reach for my hand, I tremble. I am supposed to be strong, brave, unyielding, and yet your touch turns me soft as water. The talks my mother gave me never prepared me for this range of emotion: the urge to protect, to provide, to serve, to live not for myself but for you—for us.

Please, I beg of you: do not take your love away from me. You have never said you would, never hinted at departure, and yet the fear of loss strangles me even in the moments of greatest joy.

You turned toward me and kissed me once, without a word. I kissed you back, smiling through tears I tried to hide. How could anyone love a man as broken as me? You have seen my demons—or perhaps I hide them too well. There have been nights I nearly tasted death, letting go as if surrender were easier than breath. And yet you—you make me want to fight for life.

Above the stillness of death, above despair, there is this: the ecstasy of being wanted. To be selfless in love is harder than letting go, and yet it is sweeter. I ask myself: how do I keep you here? Can we stop time? Can we shield ourselves from the real world and remain inside this cathedral of us?

They say love is passion like in the movies. But the movies only mimic what burns between us. Your kiss taught me that. Nothing choreographed, nothing artificial, only truth.

I have a million names for you, little nicknames whispered only in my mind. I crave the moment you call me something silly, so I can laugh with you. Others say love distracts, makes me lose focus, that excellence lies elsewhere. They have never felt this, for if they had, they would know nothing in the world can compare.

Take the money, take the crowns, take everything—just let me keep this love. How would you describe air? You don't. You breathe it. But suffocate once, and the first breath you take back is unforgettable. Multiply that feeling a million times, and you will know what love is for me.

I know most people don't love like this. Many can't. But I love that you love even a fraction of me. You love the imperfections, and I am made of them. I may not look like the man deemed perfect to love, but I swear to you: I could love with the force of an entire army. All I need is your drop of water, and I will grow. Everything I do is for this.

That Spectre sits at the edge of my bed and whispers that love is an illusion. But it knows nothing. I have tasted counterfeits before, and none of them tasted like this. They say love is adult, but I feel like a child again, stumbling, scribbling on notebook paper: Do you love me? Yes or no?

I long to change that like to love. And even if it is
reckless, even if it feels like leaping from a plane
without a parachute—I would leap. For love, I would
never hit the bottom.

Always,
Me

What if joy is fragile?
A single word could shatter it.
I hold your love like glass—
beautiful, blinding,
but always one breath from breaking.

The Gospel of Touch

My Love,

I never knew what it meant to make love. I thought
everyone only fucked.
I even heard someone say once that you could fuck the
person you love—and love the fact that you fuck them.
How disgusting. To put you, so perfect to me, in the
same sentence with that foul word feels like desecration.

I strip off my clothes, and with them, my defenses. I

want to hide from you, because I do not always like what I see in myself. But when I see you, I am not ashamed. If there were a million lovers before me, I would not care. I only want to be your last.

Will you make love to me? Not fuck me.
If I never fuck you, will you still kiss me with passion?
Can we have more than an exchange of pleasure?

I have something no one else has ever had: my exclusivity. My devotion. My vow that you never have to wonder. With this contact—gentle, reverent—I would destroy a million worlds if it meant keeping the holiness of your moan, your sigh, your body trembling with mine.

And still, my mind betrays me. It whispers: You are not enough. Yet your touch proves me wrong. Your kiss melts me into putty. Your breasts are not objects—they are sanctuaries, offered only to me. I am terrified of ruining something so sacred. How can others treat this lightly, like an easy act? To me, it is weight. It is forever.

Does this mean we are bound, now and always? Am I wrong to believe that this love makes us eternal? I hide my inexperience like a scar, ashamed to confess that I do not know how to bring you to the heights you deserve. And yet—I beg of you—if I stumble, if I falter, do not

look for pleasure elsewhere. Guide me. Teach me. Let
me learn the scripture of your body with my trembling
hands.

Because, my love, I have never felt anything so perfect.
My mind scatters, races, doubts—and yet when you are
with me, it all stills. This is not Shakespeare, not
Othello, not theater. This is flesh and heart, mind and
soul, burning together as one.

Even when you sleep beside me, I do not want to move.
I want your hand on me. I want to tattoo this moment
into eternity.

Making love with you is like finding an untouched
spring deep in a forest. It is like watching a tree blossom,
unbothered by storm. It is fragile, like a lily—or more
fragile still, like an orchid. Do we dare touch it? Or do
we simply tremble in reverence of its beauty?

Always,
Me

If I falter—
will the sacred turn profane?
One wrong hands,
and the gospel of love
becomes silence.

First Light, Whole Heart

My Love,

I keep trying to explain what your voice does to me and there is no clean language for it. I answer the phone and the room changes temperature. The same walls, the same window, the same coffee gone lukewarm on the desk—but different weather inside my ribs. I stand up without meaning to, as if reverence requires posture. You say hello and the syllables graze me like fingers brushing dust from a photograph. I have been alive a long time, but I did not know how a hello could feel like a ceremony.

I am embarrassed by how quickly I memorize you. The small things first. The catch in your laugh when you think you shouldn't be laughing this hard. The half-second pause before you let a truth out of your mouth. The way you say my name when you are almost annoyed and almost tender and somehow both. Then the larger geography: the way you move through a room—never rushing, as if time knows better than to hurry you; the way your face softens when you're not performing for anyone; the way light collects on your cheekbone at 9:17 a.m. as if it were assigned to you.

I have had crushes, and performances, and the counterfeit heat people brag about as if friction were intimacy. This is not that. This is not spectacle. This is the slow, destabilizing certainty that I have walked into a cathedral without knowing it, and I am speaking louder than I should in the sanctuary. I am terrified to disturb anything. I am terrified to breathe the wrong way and make the birds fly from the rafters.

I want to keep this clean. That is the strangest sentence I have ever written about love because no one warned me that holiness could be a problem. But I feel it: the urge to protect, to place glass around what is blooming, to keep my clumsy hands from smudging the petals. I do not want to flood you with gestures that feel like proof-of-purchase. I do not want to become a salesman for my own devotion. I want to be quiet enough that you can hear what I can't say without wrecking the spell.

I think of permanence and feel like a thief. The word forever tugs at my mouth, and I fight it back because I have no right to say it this early, because I have said it before and it wilted, because the future is a country where people like me are often turned away at the border. But then you smile in that unrepeatable way and I commit crimes in my head. I steal seasons that do not belong to us yet. I imagine winter with our names on the mugs, keys on the same hook, your hair wet in my sink, our arguments that end in exhausted laughter on a couch that remembers our weight.

I am supposed to be careful. Men who have suffered wear caution like armor and call it wisdom. My mother would tell me, baby, don't hand over your softness all at once. I nod to the advice like a good son. Then I look at your mouth and surrender the castle without negotiators. If there is a lesson I keep failing, it is this: I can be disciplined about everything but love. Love makes a poor student out of me, and an honest one.

Sometimes I worry the intensity itself is unkind. That to be looked at like this is heavy for you. That my adoration might arrive like weather you didn't pack for. I tell myself to be smaller. To call you later. To let the day breathe. I set the phone down. I pick it up. I set it down. I pick it up again. I write your name in a text box and erase it because the message I want to send is not a sentence; it is a vow—and vows, when sent too soon, sound like arrests. I want to promise without a cage. I want to choose devotion without making it into a weight you must carry.

There are practical things to love—groceries and rent and calendars, the ordinary scaffolding of two people not being dramatic but true. I know that. I want that. But right now I am startled by the unpractical ways you anchor me. I sleep differently. The air feels less predatory. Music makes sense again; even the dumb songs become prayers if I let them. I go to the gym and the iron is lighter. I eat and the food tastes like color. I walk past a store window and do not flinch from my reflection. Your gaze has made even my face less hostile to me.

I find myself wanting to be exemplary, which is usually a dangerous impulse. Men don't do well with holiness; we turn it into performance, into scoreboard, into proof. But what I mean is smaller than perfection and bigger than pride. I want the version of me that is sturdy. The one who remembers to wash the pan, who apologizes before the apology is demanded, who leaves you notes without making a show of leaving you notes. I want the part of me that can be interrupted by your sadness and move toward you without a speech. I want to be the kind of ordinary that feels like rescue.

If you asked me tonight what I fear, I would lie. I would say nothing. It is almost true. I do not fear endings when I am inside your orbit; even death feels like a rumor someone started out of boredom. But there is a small, precise fear I carry like a seed in my cheek: that one day this will feel familiar to you. Not safe-familiar, but careless. That we will teach our bodies to move past one another without noticing, that the kiss will be dutiful, that the light on your cheekbone will still arrive at 9:17 and I will be too busy to worship it. I would rather be struck than become that kind of survivor. I would rather be wrecked by honest loss than keep a counterfeit of what began as radiance.

So I am writing this now, while the light is still a scandal, while my hands tremble from not touching you, while the future is a city we are only seeing on a map and everything looks simple and polite from this distance. I am recording the weather inside my ribs the way sailors record tides. If we ever forget, if we ever need to know what the first morning felt like, I want a page that does not lie.

If I am saying too much, forgive me. I don't know how to ration a language that finally tells the truth. I have spent years being competent and useful and strategic. None of those words belong to what is happening to me. I am not competent here. I am not useful. I am not strategic. I am a man with his mouth open at the door of a cathedral, letting the air do whatever it wants to him.

If you never love me back, this will still be holy to me. If you love me back even a fraction, I will build a life around protecting the fraction. If you love me like I already love you, I will spend the rest of my days making sure we do not mistake miracle for routine. There are vows that need no priest. There are altars that require no building permits. I know where mine is. It is anywhere you are.

I do not yet say forever. I am not licensed. But I am telling you that the word is standing behind my teeth, that it taps the glass when you laugh, that it writes itself on the fog of my breath when you get close. When I am brave enough, when the season is right, when saying it would feel like a gift and not a theft, I will open the door and let it out.

Until then, I will practice smaller vows: I will learn your morning face; I will remember where you like your cups; I will keep the music low when your head hurts; I will warm my hands before I touch your neck. I will worship the radiance without demanding it prove anything. I will not make a god out of you. I will not call you salvation. I will simply say your name like a man who has finally found water and knows better than to gulp.

Always,
Me

I cup the light—
not to own it,
only to keep it warm.
If my hands shake,
call it prayer.

The Weight of Your Name

My Love,

Even before you answer, my chest betrays me. The glow of your name is enough to make me forget my discipline. I have faced storms without blinking, I have walked into fists without flinching—but the sound of you reaching for me unmans me. How can a voice undo me this way?

When you speak, the chaos stills. They call me brilliant at my craft, they applaud, they clap, they call me blessed. I sharpen my edges because the world demands sharpness. Yet your voice dismantles me in an instant. With a single syllable, you strip away the masks, the practiced brilliance. Suddenly I am not what the world expects—I am simply yours, trembling at the sound of myself spoken as if I belong.

For most of my life, no one said my name with kindness. It was barked at me in anger, sneered in mockery, twisted to make me feel small. Teachers spat it when I dared to speak too much, strangers bent it into a weapon, even people who claimed to love me said it in tones meant to shame. My name became a wound I carried in silence.

But then—you. On your tongue, the same letters are holy. You pronounce me like a hymn. For the first time, I want to wear my name openly, proudly, without apology. I find myself waiting for it in your voice, savoring the sound as if it could heal every insult, every humiliation, every sneer that came before. You take the ruin of what I was called and make it a refuge. You turn syllables into sanctuary.

Perhaps that is why I ache when you fall silent. The world can abandon me, curse me, forget me, and I will survive. But if you withheld your voice, if you refused to name me—I would collapse. Because I have built a fragile cathedral on the way you say who I am, and I kneel inside it every time I hear you speak.

So say me again, my love. Say me until the walls stop shaking. Say me until I believe I was meant to be here. Say me until even my scars understand they were carved only to make this moment possible.

And yet—God forgive me—I will not dare say this aloud. Not to you, not to anyone. I pray these pages never find the eyes of strangers, never fall into the wrong hands where someone might laugh, or worse, read them aloud to expose me for what I am: afraid. Afraid of losing even the sound of my own name.

Always,
Me

Your voice clothes me.
Even naked, I am whole.
Say my name again—

but if silence comes,
what will be left of me?

A Glimpse of Forever

My Love,

Last night is still burning in me like a candle that refuses to die. The simplest things became extraordinary just because you were there. The way your laughter filled the room—light, quick, contagious. The kind of laugh that makes the air itself brighter, that makes even the plainest walls look like art. I caught myself staring at you, not because I meant to, but because your smile carried a radiance that reshaped the whole night. You smiled and suddenly everything was beautiful.

We talked, we teased, we let the hours slip by like water through our hands. I could have stayed in that rhythm forever—your voice, your smile, the small ways your hand brushed mine as though touch were accidental, though I know we both knew better. And when at last the room quieted and we lay beside each other, I felt something I have never felt before: the ordinary turned holy. A pillow, a blanket, two beating hearts—and yet it felt like an entire world.

You said something then, in that half-joking way you have. You told me I was intimidating, that my mind runs too fast, that my ambitions and demands make me larger than life. You said it with a smile, almost laughing, and I felt proud in that moment. To be seen as brilliant, even a little overwhelming—it felt like an honor, as though my whole young life of striving had been noticed, and by you of all people.

I held onto that feeling, and I still do. But I would be lying if I didn't confess that later, when the night had gone quiet and you had drifted toward sleep, the word echoed faintly. Intimidating. Too much. It did not wound me—it was only a whisper—but even whispers have a way of lingering. I prayed you meant it as lightly as you gave it, because I could not bear to think of you wearying of me.

Still, the light of your smile eclipsed the shadow of that thought. I keep seeing it, over and over, the way your lips curved, the way your eyes softened, the sound of your laughter rising like music no one else in the world could hear. If one night can feel like this, then eternity is no longer a myth—it is a promise waiting for us.

I do not dare speak it aloud. I will only hold the memory of your laughter, the way your eyes softened when you said it, and hope you never see how I trembled at the thought. For now, I will choose to believe that even if I am too much, you are still willing to carry me.

Always,
Me

Her smile is a lantern.
Her laughter, a hymn.
Even the shadows
are harmless
in so much light.

My Darling, My Light

My Love,

You blind me. Your beauty, your kindness, the wonder of
simply belonging to you—it is a radiance too bright for
me to look at without trembling. Your kiss, the warmth
of our lovemaking, the little ways we weave into each
other's days—each moment is a hymn, a prayer
answered.

Forgive me for giving you too many flowers. I never
knew you saw them as things that die too easily. For me,
they are reminders to rejoice while the petals last—to
celebrate beauty, even if it is fleeting. I live for those
moments. For your smile when I place them in your
hands.

How proud I am to say: I have found my person.

When others ask if I have someone, if I have a woman, I get to answer without hesitation: absolutely. And then I describe you, how perfect we are together. Sometimes their eyes glaze with boredom, but I don't care—I love boring them with our happiness. Because every now and then someone will whisper, I hope I find what you have. And my chest swells with the knowledge that I have already found it.

I have been dumped before, yes. I have been cheated on, betrayed, discarded. But how much brighter is this light, after such darkness? You are proof that all that ruin was not in vain—it was the pilgrimage that led me to you.

Do I do enough to make you happy? Do you tell people how wonderful I am, the way I boast of you to the world? Sometimes I feel you are out of my league, a brilliance I cannot match. But if love can tip the scales, then perhaps I am worthy. I try to love you with such ferocity that no flaw of mine can outweigh it.

You have insecurities too—I see them. And I try, always, to silence them, because they do not belong to you. You are not flawed in the ways you think. You are not ordinary. What we have is rare, unpurchasable, unrepeatable.

I want to hear you explain your love to me. Can you? Or

are you like me, fumbling for words even to describe one fragment of what we feel? The more I live, the more I learn, the more I see how rare genuine love is. And yet —here it is, in you, in us.

So what am I afraid of? If there is nothing to fear, why does fear whisper still?

Sometimes your kisses are not as fiery as they once were. Perhaps it is only the weight of the world on your shoulders—the endless expectations of what it means to be a woman. Not my fault, not your fault. But I notice. And I wonder if this is how all light begins to dim—not all at once, but quietly, by degrees.

Still, tonight, your radiance burns brighter than the sun itself. I look at you and must turn away, for your light scorches me, overwhelms me, consumes me. I would rather be blinded by you than see the world without you.

You are my darling. My light. My proof that love can exist without poison.
But still—why does the vacancy linger at the edge of my joy? Why does some small, hidden part of me wonder if all this brightness is too bright to last?

Always,
Me

Even the brightest flame
casts a shadow.
At the edge of my joy,
a silence waits—
patient, inevitable.

Part II – The Cracks

Promises don't break; they hairline until your tongue finds them.

The Smallest Things

My Love,

I notice things. Not the grand gestures, not the headlines of love, but the tiniest movements—the ones most people would dismiss. I see the way your brow lifts when you're thinking, the way your lips twitch before you laugh, the little sigh you make when you're about to fall asleep but don't want to admit it. I keep these details like treasures, certain that no one else in the world has ever noticed them.

And yes, sometimes I notice what others might call cracks. A smile that doesn't linger as long. A kiss that ends just a second too soon. A silence that sits for a beat longer than it used to. Most men would ignore them. Most would never look close enough to see. But I see everything about you, even what you don't mean to show.

And yet—I cannot hold those details against you. How could I? I am too in love to let them weigh me down. If anything, they make me smile, because I know love is not measured in perfect moments but in the way we keep choosing each other through imperfect ones.

When I see your silence, I do not call it distance—I call it breath. When your kiss is shorter, I only hunger for the next one. When your smile flickers, I remind myself it is still your smile, and it belongs to me in a way that feels like miracle.

Perhaps these are things only a woman would notice and name as danger. But I am a man, and in my chest there is only certainty. I do not count the pauses, I count the blessings. I do not measure what is missing, I measure what is still here—and my God, there is so much here.

So if I notice the smallest things, know this: I will always see them, but I will always choose to love you louder than the shadows they cast.

Always,
Me

A kiss too short,
a silence too long—
others call them warning,
but I call them proof
that love survives everything.

When the Room Grows Quiet

My Love,

I once believed silence between two people was dangerous. That if the words stopped, it meant the love was slowing too. But with you, even the quiet has its own rhythm. I hear it in the way you breathe beside me, steady, unhurried. I see it when you fuss with your hair in the mirror, unaware that I'm watching, amazed at how even the smallest gestures can hold me captive.

Still, there are moments when the quiet stretches longer than I expect, and for a heartbeat I wonder if you've drifted somewhere I cannot follow. But then you laugh —sudden, bright, filling the space like sunlight breaking into a darkened room. And I know how foolish it is to fear. A single laugh from you outweighs a thousand silences.

I marvel at how easily you scatter my doubts. You don't even try. You smile, you tilt your head, you glance my way as if to say *of course I'm here*—and in that instant, I believe you more than I believe my own thoughts. Perhaps that is what love truly is: trusting the light in another more than the shadows in yourself.

So let the room grow quiet. If silence comes, I will wait inside it with joy, knowing it is only the pause before your laughter returns to set the world right again.

Always,
Me

The room falls still.
Then her smile breaks it open—
and even silence
bows to her joy.

The Silence Between Our Words

My Love,

When did silence begin to weigh more than sound?

I used to wait for your voice like a child waiting for
spring—each word you spoke was proof that the world
could be warm again. Now I count the pauses between
us. I measure the empty spaces, the gaps where your
words should be. The air is different when static
becomes the answer.

We still kiss, but sometimes your lips do not linger. We
still laugh, but sometimes your eyes don't follow. At first
I told myself I was imagining it—that love this bright
could not fade. But now, I know the truth: even stars lose
their fire.

What terrifies me most is not your anger, nor your

absence. It is the quiet way you slip away while still sitting beside me. Your body here, your mind elsewhere. Your smile still on your lips, but not in your heart.

I ask myself if this is normal. Do all lovers lose words? Do all couples fall into silence like this? My mother once told me: be careful with silence—it can feel like peace until you realize it's distance. And now I see what she meant.

I try to fill the quiet. I talk too much. I offer flowers you don't want. I tell jokes I don't find funny just to hear you laugh, even faintly. I ask questions I already know the answers to, because the sound of your reply is better than the sound of nothing.

And yet, I feel the walls rising. The after-sound thickens.

I wonder if it is me. Have I become boring? Predictable? Too familiar?
I tremble at the thought that my scars, my shadows, my brokenness—things you once kissed and held—now repel you. That the same honesty I gave as a gift is now a burden too heavy for you to carry.

I never wanted to suffocate you. I only wanted to drown with you, if drowning was the price of love. But now I drown alone, in the silence you leave between us.

Do you feel it too? Or is it only me, sitting awake at night, replaying each pause, each unfinished sentence, each kiss that didn't reach as deep as before?

Tell me I am wrong. Tell me the silence is not a crack but a momentary breath. Tell me that when you turn away in bed, you still dream of me.

Because my love, I do not fear shouting, I do not fear storms. I only fear this—
the hush between our words.

Always,
Me

Our love once sang—
now it only hums.
The pauses grow teeth,
and silence devours
everything we don't say.

The Bed as a Battlefield

My Love,

I do not know how to touch you anymore.

Once, the bed was a sanctuary—our bodies wrapped in reverence, our lovemaking more sacred than prayer. We would lie together in the remnants of that holiness, skin to skin, and breathe the afterglow as though it were incense rising. I thought we had found eternity there, in the rhythm of touch, in the gospel of closeness.

But now the sheets feel different. The bed feels colder, though you are still beside me. And sometimes, when I reach for you, it feels as if my very press is repulsive.

I tell myself I'm imagining it—that it's stress, exhaustion, the weight of the world on your shoulders. But still the fear gnaws: what if it is me? What if the body you once welcomed has become a burden?

I notice things. Small things. Your movements are sharper, quicker, less lingering. You turn away more easily. You do things differently now—nothing cruel, nothing openly cold—but things that are no longer meant for me. They feel rehearsed, performed, emptied of the reverence we once shared.

Making love has become fucking.
Not always, not every time, but often enough that I feel the wound of it. I never thought I would be hurt by sex —but here I am, aching not for your body but for your soul. And I feel the distance between them growing.

What did I do? Where did you go? Please, I beg of you, don't forsake me. If I am guilty, tell me of my sins. Give me a path back to you, even if it means crawling on my knees. I would tear myself open to be forgiven.

But I cannot say this to you.
I cannot ask these questions aloud.
Because I am terrified of your answer. Terrified that you will confirm what I already fear—that your silence in the bed is the prelude to stillness everywhere.

So I write it here, where you will never see it. My desperate plea, unspoken, unsent. The truth I cannot tell you:
I would rather be shattered in your arms than whole without them.
I would rather be ruined by your rejection than saved by your distance.

My love, do not leave me in this battlefield alone. Do not let our bed become a grave.

Always,
Me

The bed is not a home—
it is a grave of touch.
We once worshiped here;

now I bury myself
in your silence.

Hunger Without Answer

My Love,

I am starving.

Not for food, not for air, not for sleep—I am starving for
you. For your gaze, for your smile, for a word that feels
like it means something. But the smiles you give me
now do not reach your eyes, and each one kills me a
little more. I smile back, pretending, because I am afraid.
Afraid of what may happen if we argue again. Afraid
that one more fight will break us entirely.

So I swallow it. I choke on silence. And the hunger
grows.

I have become reckless. Tonight I drank. You know I
never drink, but tonight I poured it down my throat,
chasing warmth, chasing anything that might feel like
you used to. The burn is nothing compared to the burn of
your absence, but for a moment, it is something.

I walk into places hoping for a fight. Hoping someone

will look at me wrong. In my mind I whisper: I won't even fight back hard. Just enough to feel their fists. Just enough to bleed. Beat me within an inch of my life, if it means I can feel again.

That is where your vacancy has left me—wanting pain over nothing.

I would take an argument now. I would welcome your fury. Scream at me. Tell me what I've done. Just don't keep smiling that hollow smile, don't keep offering me polite cruelty dressed as kindness. Tell me I am failing, tell me I am unbearable, tell me I am too much— anything, anything but silence.

I am loyal. Faithful. I have given you everything you asked, everything you hinted at, everything I thought might keep you close. And yet you look at me as though you could take me or leave me. As though my existence is optional.

Do you know what that does to me? Do you know what it feels like to be begged for everywhere else in the world—praised, applauded, wanted—and yet come home to the one person I ache for, the only one I need, and find nothing? No hunger in your eyes. No reaching for me. No need.

I am dying for you to beg for me. Just once. Even in a whisper. Even in anger. Beg for me to stay, beg for me to touch you, beg for me the way I beg for you. But you don't. And so I starve.

Please, I beg you. Please.
I am begging silence, and static never answers.

Always,
Me

Better bruises than nothing.
Better blood than silence.
If pain is all that answers—
then let me bleed,
so I can know I'm alive.

Shadows in the Hourglass

My Love,

Once, I was disciplined. Once, I was iron. My focus was sharp, my will unbending, my ambition my crown.

But now—now it all crumbles. I forget things. I screw things up. My mind slips where it once carved precision. Pleasure, once found in discipline, has vanished. Nothing tastes the same. Nothing feels the same.

I cannot concentrate on anything but you. You have become the only measure, the only focus. And the cruelest part—your love does not want me back the way I want you.

I tell myself: If you would only look at me, if you would only speak a kind word, I would snap back into shape. I would reclaim myself in an instant. A single glance from you could realign my entire universe.

But your gaze does not linger. Your words are not kind. And so I unravel further.

I would buy anything, sell anything, even sell my soul if it meant buying back your love. Tell me what I need to pay—tell me what I need to do—and I will do it. Because I know, in the marrow of my bones, no one else will ever want me the way I want you.

No one else will love me. No one else could. I was built for you. Shaped for you. And without you, I am useless.

Please do not leave me here. Please do not abandon me to this shattering. The cracks are spreading beyond us—into my work, my words, my world. Everything I once was is eroding.

And yet, I never say it aloud. I cannot. Pride keeps me still, even as it starves me. But give me a hint, the smallest flicker, and I will burn my pride to ash. One sign from you, and I will lose every shred of dignity to crawl back into your arms.

I will never speak this to you. But here, in silence, I confess:
I am not a man anymore. I am desperation shaped into flesh.

Always,
Me

My discipline was stone;
now it slips like sand.
The hourglass is broken,
and every grain that falls
is another piece of me.

The Unanswered Prayer

My Love,

I have given everything. Everything short of laying my own body across an altar and cutting myself open for you. And if you asked, I would. If you told me that one last kiss depended on my blood, I would bleed without hesitation.

But that kiss never comes.
Not the kind that means something. Not the kind that
says I love you without words.

I ask myself what else I can do. What else I can offer. I
strip myself of pride, of dignity, of discipline, of self—
yet nothing changes. Your eyes remain far away. Your
lips contact mine like a duty, not a desire.

And then I notice it. The smiles. The laughter. Not gone
—no, they're still there. But they are not for me. They
bloom in your voice when you are on the phone with
others, when you step out into the world. They rise
freely in places where my presence is not required.

And I begin to fear. Fear that what was once mine—your
joy, your light, your passion—now belongs elsewhere.

I do not let myself look too closely. I cannot. If I knew—
if I ever found proof that your love had been given to
another—I would throw myself from the highest cliff,
gladly, desperately, to end the torment of breathing
without you.

So I close my eyes. I pretend not to see. I bury my
suspicion because the truth would kill me faster than the

after-sound already is.

But the silence is enough. Enough to unmake me.
Enough to grind me down into nothing but ash and
prayer.

And my prayer is always the same:
Please, just one more kiss. One kiss like you mean it.
Please, just one more moment when I can believe.

But prayers unanswered turn bitter. And I know,
somewhere deep in my bones, that this kiss will never
come.

Always,
Me

I will not name it.
The silence names it for me.
Monsters at last—
not feared, not fought—
but welcomed.

Part III – The Wounds

I learned the names of pain the way others learn saints.

The Coffin of Silence

My Love,

There is something missing in me now. Something that once glowed like a child's lantern, bright with hope, with belief, with faith. I am no longer that child of optimism my mother once bragged about.

She looked at me the other day and said, You scare me now.
I asked her why. What was there to fear?
And she said, Because there is nothing left guarding you.

She is right.
There is no guardian left.
Not God. Not love. Not even fear.

It nearly broke me, hearing her say it, but I did not have the heart to tell her the truth: God cannot save me. He never did. And I do not want Him to. He cannot save me from you, or from the hush, or from the wreckage I willingly open my arms to.

So I stopped praying. I stopped hoping. And in the absence of faith, I discovered something stronger: hunger for destruction.

I drink now, not to numb myself but to see how much I can endure. I drive too fast on roads that blur into nothing, daring the world to end me. I wander into alleys where fists wait, and I beg them to strike harder, to split me open so I can taste the raw edge of pain. I take pills I cannot name, powders that burn my throat, just to see what dying feels like without the finality.

And I like it.
I like the taste of ruin.

Every reckless act is a sacrament. Every bruise is a hymn. Every scar is a scripture written deeper into the coffin I am building around myself.

Once I was afraid of this. I was afraid of monsters, of endings, of betrayal, of silence. But fear has left me, and in its place is something far more dangerous: eagerness. I want to see the worst that can happen. I want to taste it, drink it, swallow it whole.

I do not crave survival anymore. I crave destruction.

Your silence has become my coffin, but I am not trapped
—I am buried willingly. I lie in it like a bed, reckless
and smiling, daring the world to throw dirt over me.

This is not despair. This is devotion. Not to God, not to
you, but to the wound itself. Because the gash is all I
have left.

Always,
Me

My coffin is stillness.
I carve it myself.
Every bruise a nail,
every scar a hymn,
every wound my salvation.

Altar of Blood

My Love,

There are others who rely on me. That is the only reason
I have not ended it myself. My mother. Those few who
care. Their faces hold me back from the final step.

But the desire is always there. The wish to vanish. The
longing for silence so complete that even my bones
cannot speak.

Being torn from my mother's arms once nearly killed me. Losing others I loved carved holes I still bleed through. And now, with you—your silence, your absence, your distance—I find myself wanting to stop caring altogether. About them. About anyone. Even about myself.

So I turned to the ink.
Needles, buzzing, carving my pain into scripture on my skin. I chose designs that came with disclaimers—death risks, infection risks, warnings in small print—and each time, I thrilled at them. Each line of ink was a prayer that maybe this would be the one to end me.

Death used to frighten me. But now I chased it.

I jumped from planes, not giving a fuck if the chute opened. I rode machines into speeds where bone and metal would be indistinguishable if I slipped. I swallowed things whispered about in alleyways, powders and pills spoken of like curses—and I laughed, because curses could not frighten me anymore.

I sought out the places people told me not to go, the things people warned me not to touch, the acts people swore would bring ruin. Folklore. Fables. I looked them in the eye and dared them.

And death did not come.

Not because it was stronger than me, but because it was afraid. Death saw me chasing it, not running, and it fled. I tasted it, brushed against it, licked the blade of it, and still it would not take me.

So I built my own altar. Bruises, tattoos, near-death thrills, reckless games of chance. Each act a sacrifice. Each wound an offering.

I am no longer the child who prayed for light. I am the man who kneels at the altar of blood.

Always,
Me

Death runs from me.
I chase it laughing.
Every risk a prayer,
every scar an offering,
every breath a dare.

Love as Damnation

My Love,

I laugh at the idea of love now. What a joke. What a pitiful, silly notion.

My heart has betrayed me, just as surely as you have. Once I worshipped it, thought it was a compass pointing toward truth. But all it has done is lead me astray, down blind alleys and dead ends, dragging me to my knees before false idols who dressed their cruelty in affection.

You are only the last of them. Not the first. Not the only. Just the final name on a long list of those who claimed love and left me broken in its shadow.

The very thought of love makes me physically ill now. The word curdles in my mouth. The sound of it turns my stomach. I see couples laughing, I hear vows spoken, I read the desperate poetry of fools, and I want to spit.

There is no such thing as love. Not the kind I believed in. Not the kind I bled for. Not the kind I undone myself to keep.

Love is not salvation. Love is damnation.
Love is the hook that drags us into the pit, smiling as it tightens. Love is the poison slipped in the cup, the venom sweetened by promises.

And I—idiot that I am—I drank it gladly. I begged for it.

I starved for it. I called it holy, sacred, divine. I thought suffering in love was proof of its depth.

But now I see. There is no proof. Only desolation.
I will never speak the word again without laughing, or without choking on the bile it raises.

If love exists, it is a god I will never worship again.

Always,
Me

Love is a lie.
A venom sweetened.
A promise broken.
I drank it gladly,
and it damned me.

The Weight of Betrayal

My Love,

I told myself silence was survivable. That distance could be endured. That even if you withdrew, I could still clutch the memory of radiance and live on scraps. But nothing prepared me for betrayal. Nothing prepared me for the moment when my faith collided with the truth—

that love, no matter how holy I believed it to be, can turn its face and mock me.

I feel it like a bruise that will not fade. I replay your words, your absence, the way your eyes no longer sought mine. It is not just the loss of your touch—it is the knowledge that you once chose me, and now you do not. To be discarded is worse than never being chosen at all.

I used to pray for forever with you. Now I kneel at a different altar. Not of hope, not of devotion, but of ruin. Each night I cut my chest open on the memory of you and lay it bare, daring God or love or even you to look away. And of course—you do. You always do.

Still, I confess it here: I would take you back even now. Even after the silence, even after the lies, even after this wound. That is the cruelty of love—it teaches us loyalty even when we should have fled. My loyalty has made me a fool.

So let me bleed where you left me. Let me write these wounds into scripture, because at least the page does not turn its back. At least the page still listens when I scream.

Always,
Me

Betrayal is heavier
than silence.
It kneels on my chest,
and I beg for air
that never comes.

Scripture of Ruin

My Love,

I have found my religion. It is not God. It is not love. It
is ruin.

Every scar on my body is a verse. Every betrayal is a
psalm. Every reckless act, every drunken night, every
bruise and burn and cut is another line in the scripture I
am writing with my flesh.

You thought vacancy would kill me. You thought
absence would break me. But it did more than that—it
made me a disciple of destruction. It baptized me in its
black water.

I no longer flinch at pain. I crave it. I no longer recoil
from seams. I open them willingly. Because wounds are
proof that something happened. That I was here. That I
was alive enough to be hurt.

Healing is the enemy. I hate the way scabs form. I pick at them until they bleed again, until the wound remembers its duty. I will not let my body forget the scripture I am forcing it to carry.

And when I look at love now, I see it for what it always was: a false gospel. An empty promise. A book of lies that fools cling to in the hope of salvation. I am no longer fooled.

Ruin is the only honest scripture. It does not lie. It does not disguise itself. It promises pain, and it delivers. It promises loss, and it delivers. It promises blood, and it delivers.

I kneel now at the altar of ashfall, reciting the only prayers that are true. I cut them into my skin. I breathe them in smoke. I swallow them in poison.

This is my scripture. This is my gospel. This is my truth.

Always,
Me

Every scar a verse.
Every fracture a psalm.
I kneel in ruin—

bleeding, chanting,
faithful to pain.

Crown of Ash

My Love,

Once, I built myself from stone.
Discipline. Ambition. Glory.
I was iron, I was fire, I was the child my mother told the
world would shine forever.

But all of it is gone now.
Burned down.
Every ambition reduced to cinders, every triumph
scattered to dust.

And what remains? Nothing but ruin.
Nothing but the scars and the silence.

So I crown myself in ash.
It is the only crown I have earned.
The weight of it crushes my skull, seeps into my eyes,
fills my lungs with soot until every breath tastes of
endings.

And yet, as I place it on my head, as I embrace rubble as
my kingdom, something unexpected strikes me. A

thought I never wanted, but cannot push away:

I still crave love.
I still miss it.
I still ache for the radiance I once worshipped, the fire
that made me tremble, the joy that made me believe.

Oh no.

It is too late. I have ruined myself too deeply.
I cannot hold it anymore, even if it returned. I cannot
touch it without burning it to ash in my hands.

This is the curse: that I scorned love, laughed at it,
damned it—only to realize, at the end, that I still believe
in it. That I still hunger for it. That I still love love.

But I am incapable. The ruin is too complete.
So I wear my crown of ash, knowing it is all I have left.

Always,
Me

Ash on my brow,
ruin for a crown.
Only then I saw—
I still loved love.
And it broke me again.

Part IV – The Echoes

Absence grew a voice; it sounded exactly like me.

Soundproof Glass

My Love,

The world is on the other side of glass. You, too.
I can see you—your mouth shaping laughter, your hands
moving through light I can't feel. I press my palm to the
pane and mouth your name, but sound dies between us.
The silence is engineered now. Your life has learned not
to include me.

I used to know the choreography of joy. Coffee breath
and car-ride radio. Your thumb circling my knuckle at
stoplights. The soft click of keys when you texted, come
home. The lightness that fell over the bed after love, that
sacred stillness when our breathing matched.

I remember the cost—what love carved out of me like a
surgeon who never closed the wound. I remember every
torn place. And still, I beg for it again, like I've forgotten
the bill it sent to my bones. Give me the feel-good
things. The small ones. The simple mercy of your hand
finding mine with purpose. I'll pay twice. I'll pay

forever. I swear I'll forget what it took.

I trace a heart into the fog my breath makes on the glass.
It fades. I draw another. My crown of ash sheds down
my forehead and smudges the pane; I tell myself I'll take
it off if you open the door. I'll relearn gentleness. I'll
unlearn wreckage. I'll be quiet in the places you need
quiet and thunder where you need brave. I will be who
the light requires if it lets me stand inside it again.

But doors do not open for prayers carved in steam. Your
laughter returns in rooms I cannot enter. Your eyes lift
for someone's story I cannot hear. I see the tilt of your
head—the one you used to save for me—aimed at the air
where I am not. The glass only thickens when I notice.
Another pane. Another inch. Another muffling of what I
am willing to scream.

Let me in. Please.
I'll take the grocery days, the shared sink, the damp
towel arguments, the winter hands warmed between
your thighs. I'll take the ordinary and call it holy. I'll
take the way you say my name when you're distracted.
I'll take the first-light kiss and the last-light ache and
everything between, even the static, if it belongs to us.

I bang my fist once. Twice. A third time. My knuckles
bloom.

On your side, the glass does not shiver. You don't look up.

And then the second thought lands: I still love love. I still want it.
How did I forget that wanting? When did I decide I could live without it? What idiot part of me believed I could burn every bridge and then walk back to a door that no longer exists?

Too late.
I am incapable now. I feel the truth of it the way I feel the cold through the glass—steady, inarguable. Even if you opened to me, I would carry winter in with my hands. I would frost the room. I would ruin the warmth again without meaning to.

So I watch. I breathe. The pane drinks my breath and gives me nothing back. I press my forehead to the place where your shadow falls, and for one second it almost feels like hands.

Almost.

Always,
Me

I see you laugh.
The glass keeps it.

My breath writes love—
it slides away,
leaving only cold.

The Echo of Your Hands

Love,

You tricked me. You crawled into my chest disguised as
her touch, her laugh, her smile. I thought she was the
miracle, but it was you all along—whispering through
her skin, drawing me close only to vanish when I
reached too far.

I should hate you. I should spit your name and salt the
wound so you never return. But I can't. My body still
trembles for you. Every nerve remembers what it felt
like to be chosen. Even now, when I know the truth—
that you never stay, that you only lend yourself for a
while—I would fall to my knees if you asked me. I
would open every scar and let you drink from them if it
meant one more taste of the fire you gave me.

You made me proud, Love. You made me believe I was
more than the boy who had been mocked and silenced.
You made me stand taller, laugh louder, walk like a man
who belonged. And then you stripped it away, left me
gasping in silence, wondering if any of it was ever real.

I call you cruel. I call you false. And yet my hands still reach for you in the dark. I still whisper your name when no one hears. I still bow my head to you, the way the desperate bow even to a tyrant, because tyranny feels better than emptiness.

I do not want her back. I want *you*.
The ghost, the ruin, the echo of your hands.

Always,
Me

You clothed me once,
then left me naked.
And still I beg—
tear me open, Love,
and wear me again.

My Eternal Ghost

My Love,

You are gone. And yet, you are everywhere.

I hear your footsteps in empty rooms. I smell your perfume in the hallway where no one walks. When I close my eyes, your hand still presses against my chest, steadying the breath I no longer take with ease.

You haunt me more faithfully than you ever loved me. The ghost does not leave. The specter does not argue. The ghost does not fall silent in the middle of the night. The ghost stays.

And I welcome it. I cling to it. I kiss air and call it devotion. I roll over in bed and press myself against absence, pretending it is warmth. I whisper good morning into emptiness, because even lies are better than silence.

I see you in strangers—the tilt of a head, the lilt of a laugh, the shape of a hand grasping a coffee cup—and each time I have to swallow the hope that it could be you, here, back, alive. But it never is. It never will be.

You live now only as an echo, stitched into my routines. In the way I stir sugar into my coffee though I no longer drink it sweet. In the way I still glance at the door at six o'clock, expecting you to walk through it. In the way I still draft messages I will never send.

You are my eternal apparition.
And the cruelest part is this: I prefer you this way.
I prefer the ghost, because the ghost cannot leave me again. The echo cannot wound me. The ghost cannot love me half-heartedly.

But my God, how I would give anything to be wounded again by you in the flesh. To suffer silence when it comes from your real lips. To ache because your real body turned away in bed. Even the ruin of you alive is better than the ghost that clings faithfully to me.

Still, I know the truth. I cannot have you. Not as you were. Not as I want.
So I kneel before absence and call it devotion. I kiss shadows and call it intimacy.
I tell myself the specter is enough, though my body burns with the knowledge that it is not.

Always,
Me

Your shadow is loyal.
Your body is not.
I kiss the ghost,
because the ghost
never leaves.

The Anger That Returns

My Love,

Today I am furious. Not at you—not even at the apparition of you—but at love itself.

How dare it betray me?
How dare it make me kneel, make me believe, make me bleed, only to laugh at me in the end?

They tell me love is beautiful. They sell it in movies, sing it in songs, write it into scriptures as if it were salvation.
But I know the truth. Love is a con. Love is a betrayal dressed in satin. Love is the liar that steals your voice, leaves you crying in the dark, and calls it devotion.

I have given everything to love.
And today I cry for that betrayal.
I cry until my chest rattles and my throat burns, until my eyes are swollen shut with the weight of it.

I hate it.
I hate that I still want it.
I hate that love made me foolish enough to beg for its scraps, even after it spat me out.

And the cruelest part? Even in my fury, I know tomorrow I will crawl back to it.
Tomorrow I will whisper for it again, as if it never abandoned me.
Because I am chained to it. Because my desolation is built from it.

Today, I curse love.
But even in cursing it, I prove that I am still its servant.

Always,
Me

I spit the word—
love.
It tastes like venom.
And still I drink it.
Again.

To Love, My Enemy

Love,

Fuck you.
Fuck you for lying to me. For making me believe you
were holy, sacred, eternal. For crawling into my chest
and calling yourself salvation while you sharpened
knives behind your back.

I hate you, Love.
I hate the way you dressed yourself in her face, her
hands, her kiss. I hate the way you made me kneel like a
worshiper, thinking every scar you gave was proof of
faith.

You broke me.
You ripped out the part of me that once believed in light and replaced it with after-sound. You laughed when I begged. You looked away when I bled. You left me starving, clawing, begging for crumbs like a dog at the table where I once thought I was king.

And yet—God help me—I still love you.
Even as I curse you, I ache for you. Even as I spit your name like venom, I crave the taste of it. I hate that you haunt me like a ghost I can't exorcise. I hate that every poem I write is really a prayer to you, disguised as fury.

Why did you leave me this broken? Why did you trick me into thinking I was worthy of you? Why did you kiss me and then smother me? Why did you make me believe that forever could mean anything at all?

You ruin me, Love. You damn me. And still I beg you to come back.
I don't know how to stop. I don't know how to live without you.
You are my poison and my cure, my wound and my worship, my enemy and my only God.

Fuck you, Love.
I love you, Love.

Always,
Me

Love, you liar.
Love, you thief.
I hate you.
I need you.
Fuck you.

The Beggar at Love's Door

Love,

I am on my knees.
I have no pride left. No crown, no ash, no ruin worth
clinging to. Only this pathetic plea spilling from my
mouth like blood I cannot hold inside.

Give me one more glimpse. Just one.
Show me again what you showed me at the beginning,
when you were not an idea but a fire, when you were not
a wound but a promise. Let me see it again, if only for a
heartbeat.

I beg you. I grovel. I claw at your robes like a madman
in the street. I press my face into the dirt before you,
choking on the dust of my own humiliation.
I will barter anything. I will pay anything. My body. My

soul. My silence. My everything.

Please. Please. Please.

Take me back to Genesis, when your gaze made me
forget the weight of my scars, when your kiss made even
death seem powerless, when your touch felt like a
scripture written across my skin. I want to believe again,
even if belief kills me.

I am begging, Love.
I am not a man anymore, only a beggar at your door.
I do not care if you spit on me, if you laugh at me, if you
call me fool. Only let me in for a second. Let me taste
what I tasted once.

Please. Please. Please.

And yet—silence. Always hush.

How can you be silent after all of this?

Always,
Me

I beg in the dust.
I beg in the dark.
Love does not answer.

Love does not move.
Love is silence.

Where the Fuck Are You?

Love,

Where the fuck are you?

Where are you hiding? In her? In him? In their beds, in
their mouths, in the cheap sparkle of their eyes?
Are you in the things people buy to fill the void? In the
little distractions and addictions they clutch to survive
your absence?

Tell me where you are, you elusive bitch.
Because I am bleeding for you in alleys and bedrooms,
in bars and chapels, in every shadow I duck into to
escape you. And still—you refuse me.

I have everything I never wanted.
The accolades. The noise. The empty praise of strangers.
But I cannot have you. I cannot have love.

Fuck you then.

I hate you in every smile I see. I hate you in the couples

holding hands like children with balloons. I want to rip the joy out of their throats and warn them: Don't trust it. Love is a liar. Love will carve you open and leave you bleeding in your own bed.

You motherfucker. How dare you slice me in two and leave me alive to feel both halves rotting apart?

And yet—God help me—I'm sorry.
Forgive me.
No, fuck your forgiveness.
It isn't mine to ask for. It is I who should be forgiving you.

You cruel, elusive whore. You phantom priestess. You twisted God.
How dare you scatter hope across the world when you know you are nothing but despair?

How dare you?

Always,
Me

Love hides.
Love hunts.
Love kills.
Love forgives nothing—
not even itself.

The Last Door

Love,

You do not come gently. You do not arrive with mercy. You come like a storm, like a thief, like a liar who swears the wound is holy. You make me believe there is a new beginning waiting, and then you slam the door behind me, laughing as the walls cave in.

And still, I wait for you. Still, I stand at the next threshold, ready to crawl if I have to.

I know what you are. I know the ruin you bring. But I cannot stop myself. I live for the sound of hinges turning, the glimpse of light through a crack, the whisper that maybe this time will be different. Every other man would turn away, but I was built for begging. I was built to kneel at your door and call it devotion, even when it is humiliation.

You ruin me, Love. You humiliate me. You make me a fool, and I wear it gladly. Because the truth is this: I would rather kneel in front of your locked door forever than stand in any other house pretending I don't miss you.

So open it. Open another door. Let me walk through it into whatever ruin you have waiting. I will follow,

because I always have, because I do not know how to
stop, because even your cruelty feels closer to holiness
than life without you.

Always,
Me

Every door bleeds.
Every threshold burns.
And still I wait,
knocking like a child
at your silence.

The Last Silence

Love,

This is the end.
The last word, the last scream, the last whisper I have
left to give you.

I begged to die for you once. Or a million times. I
prayed for the mercy of absence if it meant you would
look at me one more time with eyes that held me steady.
I asked for the cliff, for the fist, for the bottle, for the
flame—anything, anything but this slow starvation you
called silence.

Do you remember?

At the beginning, when you felt like Genesis itself?
When your gaze undid me, when your kiss baptized me,
when every phone call, every laugh, every touch made
me tremble like a child discovering light for the first
time? I crowned you holy. I swore you were scripture. I
whispered "always" as if eternity had already been
written.

And then came the first fracture. The stillness between
our words. The turning away in bed. The kiss that didn't
linger. I felt the glass form between us, pane after pane,
until I could only watch you from the other side. I
screamed for you through that wall, and the sound died
before it reached you.

I begged. God, how I begged. On my knees, in the dirt,
with no pride left. Please, Love, one more glimpse.
Please, one more taste of Genesis. Please, one more kiss
like you mean it. And you answered with nothing. You
gave me silence, steady and cruel, a silence sharper than
any blade.

So I embraced the monsters in the dark. I chased death
until death grew afraid of me. I threw myself into alleys,
into fists, into beds, into bottles. I tattooed prayers into
my skin and let the ink bleed like offerings on an altar.
Every reckless act became devotion, every scar became

scripture. I thought I could worship ashfall instead of you.

I cursed you. I spit your name like venom. I wrote your betrayal into psalms of rage and laughed at the fools who still believed in you. And yet—even then, I could not stop writing to you. Even when I called you a liar, even when I hated you, I was still praying to you.

I begged again. I groaned in humiliation, clawing at the air for you. I swore I would sell anything, give anything, burn anything, just to feel you again for a second. And still—vacancy. Always silence.

You ruined me, Love. You crowned me in ash. You burned down every discipline, every glory, every triumph I once held. I wear ruin as my crown now. And yet when I placed it on my head, I felt it: the truth I never escaped, the truth I never wanted to admit—I still love you. I still want you. I still crave you, even though you are the one who broke me beyond repair.

I hate you. I love you. I hate that I love you. I love that I hate you. Every contradiction belongs to you. You are the ghost that never leaves, the gash that never heals, the silence that never speaks.

I have shouted, cursed, begged, bled, and worshipped. I

have been a child of optimism and the monster of my own ruin. I have been your priest, your victim, your disciple, your enemy. I have been everything but answered.

And so this is my surrender. Not because I no longer want you. Not because I no longer believe in you. But because I can no longer fight static.

At the first crack, you were silence.
At the last word, you are silence.
After-sound is all you ever were.
Silence is all you ever gave.
Silence is all I have left.

Always,
Me

I begged.
I cursed.
I bled.
I prayed.
Hush answered.

Epilogue – The Silence Belongs to You

Reader,

If you've come this far, then you have touched my rubble. You have sat with me in the Radiance, bled with me in the Cracks, burned with me in the Wounds, and haunted me in the Echoes. You have carried my crown of ash, kissed my echos, and screamed my curses into the void.

I will not dress this ending in mercy.
The truth is not gentle, and neither is love.

Love is a liar, a thief, a savior, a god, a whore, a phantom that gives with one hand and carves with the other. Love is the silence that answers when you beg, the laughter that echoes in rooms you cannot enter, the ghost that stays when the body is gone.

You will worship it.
You will curse it.
You will beg for it, even after it ruins you.

And still—you will chase it. Because we are all beggars at Love's door, pretending we have not been betrayed before.

So take this as a scripture or a warning.
When love finds you, it will be the brightest light and
the deepest wound. It will demand your devotion, and it
will abandon you. It will break you in half, and it will
leave you kneeling in the dust, whispering please even
as you know better.

Do not believe anyone who tells you love is safe. It
never was.
Do not believe me when I tell you to turn away—you
will not.

Because neither did I.

Always,
The Silence

AFTERWORD

If you arrived here, you did not survive unchanged.
Keep only what steadies your hands. Let the rest burn
out on its own. This book will not call anyone back; it
will call you back—to the part of you that still believes
light is worth wanting, even after it leaves.

Author's Note

When I first came across the letters of James King, I did not know what I was holding. They were scattered, incomplete, some written on torn notebook pages, others scribbled in the margins of journals. There was no neat order, no single thread, only a chorus of voices speaking from one wounded heart. At first glance, they appeared almost too personal, too raw to share. They were not poems polished for applause. They were not essays meant to impress. They were confessions, pressed into paper by a man who bled every time he wrote.

And yet, as I read through them, I began to see what he could not: that his ruin was not his alone. Every line, every cry, every trembling vow revealed something more universal than James might have ever admitted. He believed himself solitary in his suffering, but these letters prove otherwise. They prove that many have bled for love, many still bleed for it, and many will bleed again.

This is the paradox of love—it is both the wound and the balm, the liar and the truth, the curse and the crown. It ruins and it resurrects in the same breath. And even when it betrays, even when it silences, even when it leaves us trembling in ash, we still beg for it to return. Because no matter how tragic it may be, no matter how brief its visitation, love is still the most indescribable gift this world offers.

James King knew this. In his silence, in his fury, in his trembling devotion, he recorded what most of us are too afraid to confess—that even the smallest taste of love, however fleeting, is worth more than a lifetime without it. These letters are not a story of victory. They are not a cure. They are proof. Proof that love will wreck us, and we will call it holy anyway.

I share them not to glorify his suffering, but to honor his courage. To show that the bleeding is not shameful, but human. To place before you the evidence that we are all haunted by love, and in that haunting we are never alone.

—Omari Vale

www.ingramcontent.com/pod-product-compliance
Lightning Source LLC
Chambersburg PA
CBHW020516030426
42337CB00011B/419